童言无忌

Childlike Innocence

中国国家汉办赠送 外文出版社
Donated by Hanban, China

图书在版编目（CIP）数据

童言无忌/李浸编译．—北京：外文出版社，2005（笑话集锦）
ISBN 7-119-04244-0

Ⅰ．童… Ⅱ．李… Ⅲ．英语-对照读物，笑话-英、汉
Ⅳ．H319.4：Ⅰ

中国版本图书馆 CIP 数据核字（2005）第 111150 号

外文出版社网址：
  http://www.flp.com.cn
外文出版社电子信箱：
  info@flp.com.cn
  sales@flp.com.cn

笑话集锦

童言无忌

编　　译　李　浸

责任编辑　李春英
封面设计　李迎迎
印刷监制　冯　浩
出版发行　外文出版社
社　　址　北京市百万庄大街 24 号　　邮政编码　100037
电　　话　（010）68995883（编辑部）
　　　　　（010）68329514/68327211（推广发行部）
印　　刷　三河汇鑫印务有限公司
经　　销　新华书店/外文书店
开　　本　32 开　　　　　　　　字　数　30 千字
印　　数　5001—10000 册　　　印　张　5.625
版　　次　2006 年第 1 版第 2 次印刷
装　　别　平
书　　号　ISBN 7-119-04244-0
定　　价　9.80 元

目 录
Contents

Black or White?

A little girl at a wedding asked, "Mommy, why do brides always wear white?"

"Because they're happy," the mom replied.

Halfway through the wedding, the girl whispered, "Mommy, if brides wear white because they're happy, then why do grooms wear black?"

黑色还是白色？

在一场婚礼上，一个小姑娘问道："妈妈，为什么新娘总是穿白色的衣服？"

妈妈答道："因为她们很高兴。"

婚礼进行到一半时，小姑娘又小声问道："妈妈，如果新娘穿白色的衣服是因为高兴，那么为什么新郎要穿黑色的衣服呢？"

☆ **whisper** /ˈhwɪspə(r)/ *v.* 低语，耳语；低声说出

3

Some Good Advice on
Life from Kids

Never trust a dog to watch your food.

When your dad is mad and asks you, "Do I look stupid?", don't answer.

Never tell your mom her diet's not working.

Don't pull dad's finger when he tells you to.

When your mom is mad at your dad, don't let her brush your hair.

Don't sneeze in front of mom when you're eating crackers.

You can't hide a piece of broccoli in a glass of milk.

If you want a kitten, start out by asking for a horse.

孩子们对于生活的忠告

绝对不能让狗狗帮你看着食物。

你爸爸气急败坏地问你"我是不是很蠢"时，不要回答。

千万不要对妈妈说她的节食没有效果。

爸爸让你拉他的手指时不要这样做。

妈妈在生爸爸的气时，不要让她给你梳头。

吃薄脆饼干时不要在妈妈面前打喷嚏。

你不可能把花椰菜藏在牛奶里。

如果你想要一只小猫，就从一匹马要起吧。

Don't pick on your sister when she's holding a baseball bat.

When you get a bad grade in school, show it to your mom when she's on the phone.

Don't flush the toilet when your dad's in the shower.

Never ask for anything that costs more than $5 when your parents are doing taxes.

When you want something expensive, ask your grandparents.

Never tell your little brother that you're not going to do what your mom told you to do.

Remember the two places you are always welcome: church and Grandma's house.

When you have something you don't need, give it to the church.

你的姐姐拿着棒球棒时，不要去惹她。

你成绩单上的分数不够好，就趁妈妈打电话时拿给她。

不要在爸爸洗澡时冲马桶。

爸爸妈妈计算税账时，不要去要求五块钱以上的东西。

想要贵的东西，就去找爷爷奶奶吧。

不想做妈妈让你做的事情时，千万不要把这个想法告诉弟弟。

记得你永远受欢迎的两个地方：教堂和奶奶家。

你不再需要的东西，就捐给教堂吧。

☆ **sneeze** /sniːz/ *v.* 打喷嚏

☆ **broccoli** /ˈbrɒklɪ/ *n.* 【植】花椰菜，球花甘蓝

☆ **flush** /flʌʃ/ *v.* 冲洗；清除

Peanuts

A zookeeper approaches three boys standing near the lions' cage and asks them their names and what they're up to.

The first boy says, "My name's Tommy and I was trying to feed peanuts to the lions."

The second boy says, "My name's Jerry and I was trying to feed peanuts to the lions."

The third boy says, "My name is Peanuts."

皮纳兹

　　动物园的一个饲养员走近三个站在狮笼边的小男孩，问他们都叫什么和来干什么。

　　第一个男孩说："我的名字是汤米，我想要把花生喂给狮子。"

　　第二个男孩说："我叫杰里，我想要把花生喂给狮子。"

　　第三个男孩说："我的名字是花生（皮纳兹）。"

　　☆ approach /əˈprəʊtʃ/ v. 靠近，接近

Where Are My Clothes?

A little girl and a little boy was admiring the famous statue by Rede entitled "The Thinker".

Girl: What do you suppose he's thinking?

Boy: I should imagine he's thinking about where he put his clothes!

我的衣服哪儿去了？

一个小女孩和一个小男孩在欣赏罗丹的著名的雕像《思想者》。

女孩：你猜他在想什么？

男孩：我认为他在想他把自己的衣服放哪儿了！

☆ **admire** /əd'maɪə(r)/ *v.* 欣赏；敬佩.

☆ **suppose** /sə'pəʊz/ *v.* 猜想；认为

11

You Coward!

One summer evening during a violent thunderstorm a mother was tucking her small boy into bed. She was about to turn off the light when he asked with a tremor in his voice, "Mommy, will you sleep with me tonight?"

His mother smiled and gave him a reassuring hug. "I can't dear," she said, "I have to sleep in daddy's room."

A long silence was broken at last by his little voice. "The big sissy!"

你个胆小·鬼！

在一个雷电交加的风雨夏夜里，妈妈给她年幼的儿子盖好被子，准备关灯时，听到他嗓音颤抖着问道："妈妈，今天晚上你能不能陪我睡呀？"

妈妈微笑着安慰地抱了抱他，说道："宝贝，我不能，我得在爸爸的房间里睡。"

沉默了好久之后，只听小男孩用微弱的声音说道："那个人胆小鬼！"

☆ **tuck** /tʌk/ *v.*（用被子）把…舒适地裹在里面

☆ **tremor** /ˈtremə(r)/ *n.* 战栗，颤抖

☆ **reassuring** /ˌriːəˈʃʊərɪŋ/ *a.* 安慰（性）的，鼓励（性）的

☆ **sissy** /ˈsɪsɪ/ *n.*〈口〉懦弱胆怯的人

They're All Busy

One day, the phone rang, and a little boy answered.

"Excuse me, may I speak with your father?"

"No, he is busy," he whispers.

"Oh. Well then, may I speak with your mother?"

"No, she is busy," the kid says softly.

"Oh. Is anybody else there?"

"The police."

"Can I speak to them?"

"They're busy."

"Oh. Is anybody else there?"

他们都很忙

一天，电话铃响，一个小男孩接听了。

"你好，能请你爸爸接电话吗？"

"不行，他在忙。"小男孩悄声答道。

"那么，能请你妈妈接电话吗？"

"不行，她也在忙。"小男孩轻轻说道。

"那么，还有别人在吗？"

"警察在。"

"可以请他们接电话吗？"

"他们在忙。"

"还有人吗？"

"The firemen."

"Can I speak to them?"

"They're busy."

"So let me get this straight — your parents, the police and the firemen are there, but they're all busy? What are they doing?"

"They're looking for me."

"消防员在。"

"能请他们接电话吗?"

"他们在忙。"

"好吧,让我把情况搞清楚——你父母、警察,还有消防员都在你家里,可是他们都在忙?他们在做什么?"

"他们在找我。"

☆ **get straight** 彻底了解（或弄清、搞懂）

17

What Would You Do?

Son: Mom, if someone broke your best vase, what would you do?

Mother: I'd spank his bottom and send him to bed without any supper!

Son: Wow, you'd better get your slipper ready. DAD has just broken it!

你准备怎么做?

儿子:妈妈,如果有人打碎了你最好的花瓶,你会怎么做?

妈妈:我要打他的屁股,而且不让他吃晚饭就去睡觉!

儿了:哇,这样啊。那你准备好拖鞋吧,爸爸刚把花瓶打碎了!

☆ spank /spæŋk/ v. (用手掌、拖鞋等) 掴,拍打 (尤指打屁股)

What Did I Say?

A family was having some guests to dinner. At the table, the mother turned to her little daughter and said, "Dear, would you like to say the blessing?"

"I wouldn't know what to say," replied the little girl, shyly.

"Just say what you hear Mommy say, sweetie," the woman said.

Her daughter took a deep breath, bowed her head, and solemnly said, "Dear Lord, why the hell did I invite all these people to dinner!?!"

我说过什么？

家里来了几位客人吃晚饭。在餐桌前，妈妈转向她的小女儿："宝贝，由你来做祷告，好不好？"

"可是我不知道说什么。"小姑娘羞涩地答道。

"你听妈妈平常说什么，宝贝，说出来就行了。"

小女孩深吸一口气，低下头，庄重地说道："上帝，我到底为什么要请这些人来吃饭呢！？"

21

Do It Again!

The parents had just finished tucking their little girl into bed one evening when they heard sobbing coming from three-year-old Billy's room.

Rushing to his side, they found him crying hysterically.

He had accidentally swallowed a penny and was sure he was going to die. No amount of talking could change his mind.

Desperate to calm him, the father palmed a penny that he happened to have in his pocket and pretended to pull it from Billy's ear.

再来一遍！

爸爸妈妈刚把小女儿送上床睡觉，就听到从三岁的比利的房间里传来抽泣声。

爸爸妈妈赶紧跑过去，小比利正在歇斯底里地哭着。

原来小比利不小心吞下了一枚硬币，他认为自己死定了。爸爸妈妈怎么安慰他都没用。

爸爸急于安抚他，兜里又正好有一枚硬币，于是他把硬币藏在手心里，假装把比利吞下去的那枚从耳朵里拉了出来。

Billy was delighted. In a flash, he snatched it from his father's hand, swallowed it and demanded cheerfully, "Do it again, Dad!"

比利很高兴。他一把从爸爸手里抓过硬币，吞了下去，兴奋地叫道："爸爸，爸爸，再来一遍！"

☆ **hysterically** /hɪˈsterɪkəlɪ/ *ad.* 情绪异常激动地；歇斯底里地

☆ **swallow** /ˈswɒləʊ/ *v.* 吞下，咽下

☆ **desperate** /ˈdespərət/ *a.* 极想望的，极需要的

☆ **palm** /pɑːm/ *v.* 把…藏于手（掌）中

☆ **in a flash** 马上，一瞬间

☆ **snatch** /snætʃ/ *v.* 夺，一把抓住

No Word about Ears

Little Johnny's next doors had a baby. Unfortunately, the baby was born without ears.

When they arrived home from the hospital, the parents invited Little Johnny's family to come over and see their new baby. Little Johnny's dad had a talk with little Johnny before going to the neighbors.

He said, "Now, son ... that poor baby was born with no ears. I want you to be on your best behavior and not say one word about his ears or I am really going to spank you when we get back home."

不能提耳朵

小约翰尼的邻居生了小孩。不幸的是宝宝生来没有耳朵。

从医院回到家后，宝宝的父母邀请小约翰尼一家过来看新生儿。在过去之前，爸爸和小约翰尼谈了一次话。

爸爸说："呃，孩子……那个可怜的婴儿生来没有耳朵。我希望你能好好表现，不要提他的耳朵。否则我们回来后，我真的会揍你一顿的。"

"I promise not to mention his ears at all," said Little Johnny.

At the neighbor's home, Little Johnny leaned over in the crib and touched the baby's hand. He looked at it's mother and said, "Oh, what a beautiful little baby." The mother said, "Thank you very much, Little Johnny."

He then said, "This baby has perfect little hands and perfect little feet. Why ... just look at his pretty little eyes.... Did his doctor say that he can see good?"

The Mother said, "Why, yes Johnny ... his doctor said he has 20/20 vision."

Little Johnny said, "Well, it's a good thing, 'cause he sure couldn't wear glasses!!!"

小约翰尼答道："我保证绝不提他的耳朵。"

在邻居家里，小约翰尼俯身在童床上，摸了摸宝宝的小手。然后转向宝宝的妈妈说："多漂亮的小宝宝啊！""太谢谢你这样说了，小约翰尼。"

他又接着说道："小宝宝长着漂亮的小手和小脚。呃……瞧瞧这对漂亮的眼睛……医生说他的眼睛没问题吧？"

宝宝妈妈答道："当然，约翰尼，医生说他的视力足有2.0。"

小约翰尼说："哦，这就好啦，因为他肯定戴不了眼镜！！！"

☆ **unfortunately** /ˌʌntfəˈtʃɔːfˌnʌɪ/ *ad.* 不幸地；倒霉地；遗憾的是

☆ **be on one's best behavior** 竭力循规蹈矩

29

Why Did You Eat Him?

A three-year-old walked over to a pregnant lady. He inquisitively ask the lady, "Why is your stomach so big?"

She replied, "I'm having a baby."

With big eyes, he asked, "Is the baby in your stomach?"

She said, "He sure is."

Then the little boy with a puzzled look asked, "Is it a good baby?"

She said, "Oh yes, its a real good baby."

With even a more surprised and shocked look he said, "Then why in the world did you eat him?"

你为什么吃了他?

一个三岁的小孩走到一位怀孕的女士跟前。他好奇地问道:"你的肚子为什么那么大?"

她答道:"我怀了一个小宝宝。"

他瞪圆了眼睛,问道:"小宝宝在你的肚子里吗?"

"是的,当然在我的肚子里。"

小男孩一脸困惑地问道:"小宝宝乖吗?"

"是的,真是个乖宝宝。"

小男孩震惊地看着她问:"那么你到底为什么要把他吃掉呢?"

☆ **inquisitively** /ɪnˈkwɪzətɪvlɪ/ *ad.* 好奇地;爱钻研地

31

Washing the Dog

A young boy walks into the corner grocery store and picks out a huge box of laundry detergent. The grocer walked over asked the boy if he had a lot of laundry detergent to do.

"Oh, no laundry," the boy said, "I'm going to wash my dog!"

"But you shouldn't use this to wash your dog. It's very powerful and if you wash your dog in this, he'll get sick. In fact, it might even kill him."

But the boy was not to be stopped and carried the detergent to the counter and paid for it.

给狗狗洗澡

一个小男孩走进街角的便利店，拎起一大袋洗衣粉。店主走过来问他是不是有一大堆的衣服要洗。

"不，没有，"小男孩答道，"我要给我的狗洗澡。"

"可是你不应该用这洗衣粉给狗洗澡，这个太强效了，你的狗会生病，甚至死掉。"

但是，小男孩不肯听劝。他把洗衣粉拿到收银台交钱走了。

About a week later the boy was back in the store to buy some candy. The grocer asked the boy how his dog was doing.

"Oh, he died," the boy said sadly.

The grocer, trying not to be an I-told-you-so, said he was sorry the dog died but added, "I tried to tell you not to use that detergent on your dog!"

"Well," the boy replied, "I don't think it was the detergent that killed him."

"Oh? What was it then?"

"I think it was the spin cycle!"

大约一星期后，小男孩又来店里买糖。店主问小男孩他的狗怎么样了。

"呃，它死了，"小男孩伤心地答道。

店主说为他很难过，又做出先知先觉的样子，说："我不让你用洗衣粉给狗洗澡来着。"

"哦，我想不是洗衣粉的问题。"

"啊？那是为什么？"

"我想是甩干程序吧！"

☆ **powerful** /'pauəful/ *a.* 效力大的；强壮的

35

My Dad Is the Best!

3 young boys were trying to figure out whose dad was the best.

"My dad is so good he can shoot an arrow, run after it, get in front of it, and catch it in his bare hands."

"My dad is so good that he can shoot a gun, run after the bullet, get in front of it and catch it in his bare hands."

"I've got you both beat. My dad's so good because he works for the state of Florida. He gets off work at 5:00 and is home by 4:30."

我爸爸是最棒的！

三个小男孩想要比出谁的爸爸最棒。

"我爸爸太棒了，他能射出一支箭，跟在箭后面跑，超过它，然后徒手抓住它。"

"我爸爸才棒呢，他能打出一发子弹，跟在后面跑，超过它，然后徒手抓住它。"

"我可要胜过你们俩了。我爸爸才牛呢，他为佛罗里达州政府工作。他 5 点下班，可 4 点半就到家了。"

What Did He Do?

Little Bobbie ran up to her mom sobbing, with her doll in her hand.

Bobbie: Mommy, Billy broke my new doll!

Mom: It's all right, dear. I'll get you a new one. By the way, how did he do that?

Bobbie: I hit him over the head with it.

他做了什么？

小博比哭着跑到妈妈身边，手里拿着她的娃娃。

博比：妈妈，比利把我的新娃娃弄坏了！

妈妈：没关系的，宝贝。我会再给你买一个。顺便问一句，他是怎么给你弄坏的？

博比：我用娃娃打他的头。

Where's My Booger?

As I was trying to pack for vacation, my 3-year-old daughter was having a wonderful time playing on the bed.

At one point, she said, "Mom, look at this," and stuck out two of her fingers.

Trying to keep her entertained, I reached out and stuck her fingers in my mouth and said, "Mommy is gonna eat your fingers!" pretending to eat them before I rushed out of the room again.

我的鼻屎干哪儿去了？

在我忙着为出去度假收拾行李的时候，我二岁的女儿在床上玩儿得很开心。

一时，她伸出两跟手指，说："妈妈，看这个。"

为了逗她玩儿，我凑过去把她的手指放到我嘴里假装吃掉："妈妈把你的手指吃掉了！"然后我就跑出了房间。

When I returned, my daughter was standing on the bed staring at her fingers with a devastated look on her face and tears down her face.

I said, "What's wrong honey?"

Sad and broken up she looked at me and said, "Mommy, where's my booger?"

等我回来的时候，我的女儿站在床上，伤心地盯着她的手指，眼泪都流下来了。

"怎么了，我的宝贝？"

她伤心欲绝地看着我说："妈妈，我的鼻屎干到哪儿去了？"

☆ devastated /'devəsteɪtɪd/ *a.* 震惊的；悲痛欲绝的

Eat Like a Horse

Little Susie was Mommy's helper. She helped set the table. Soon, everything was on, Mr. Smith, the guest came in, and everyone sat down.

Then Mother noticed something was missing . . . .

"Susie, dear," she said, "You didn't put a knife and fork at Mr. Smith's place."

"But, Mommy, I thought he wouldn't need them," explained Susie. "Daddy says he always eats like a horse!"

像马一样吃饭

小苏茜是妈妈的好帮手。吃饭前，她帮妈妈摆碗筷。很快，一切都准备好了。客人史密斯先生也来了，大家都入座。

妈妈注意到桌子上少了些东西。

"苏茜宝贝，你忘了在史密斯先生面前摆上刀叉。"

"可是，妈妈，我是想他不需要这些的，"小姑娘答道，"爸爸说他'像马一样吃饭'。"

☆ **eat like a horse** 是一句俗语，意思是"吃得很多"。

I Didn't Do My Homework

A little girl came home from school and said to her mother, "Mommy, today in school I was punished for something that I didn't do."

The mother exclaimed, "But that's terrible! I'm going to have a talk with your teacher about this ... by the way, what was it that you didn't do?"

The little girl replied, "My homework."

我没做作业

一个小姑娘放学回到家里，对妈妈说："妈妈，今天在学校里，老师为我没做过的事情罚我。"

她妈妈惊呼："这太不像话了！我得去找你们老师谈谈……哦，对了，你没做什么事情？"

小女孩答道："我没做作业。"

☆ **exclaim** /ɪk'skleɪm/ *v.* （表示抗议、责难等）大声叫嚷，激烈地表示意见

What Big Goldfish!

Little Johnny was in the garden filling in a hole when his neighbor peered over the fence.

Interested in what the cheeky little boy was doing, he politely asked, "What are you up to there, Johnny?"

"Well, my goldfish died," replied Johnny tearfully, without looking up, "and I've just buried him."

"But that's an awfully big hole for the goldfish, isn't it?"

Johnny patted down the last heap of earth then replied, "That's because he's inside your big fat cat!"

好大一条金鱼！

小约翰尼正在花园里填一个洞，这时他的邻居从栅栏那边看过来。

邻居很好奇这个冒失的小男孩在做什么，于是礼貌地问道："小约翰尼，你在做什么？"

"呃，我的金鱼死了，"小约翰尼没有抬头，哭着答道，"我刚把它埋了。"

"可是这个洞对一条金鱼来说实在是太大了，不是吗？"

小约翰尼轻轻抬平最后一堆土，答道："那是因为我的鱼在您的大肥猫肚子里。"

☆ **peer** /pɪə(r)/ *v.* 仔细看，凝视

☆ **cheeky** /'tʃiːkɪ/ *a.* 放肆的，莽撞的

☆ **tearfully** /'tɪəfʊlɪ/ *ad.* 流泪地，哭泣地

☆ **awfully** /'ɔːfʊlɪ/ *ad.* 非常地，十分

Was He Sick?

A mother went to the kitchen window to check on her three-year-old son, who was playing in the yard with some older children.

She was horrified to see that they were feeding him an earthworm.

She quickly opened the window and screamed at them, "Don't feed him worms! They'll make him sick!"

They looked up at her puzzled and asked, "Was he sick yesterday?"

他病了吗？

妈妈走到厨房窗口看她三岁的儿子，小宝宝正在花园里和一些大点儿的孩子们一块玩。

看到那些孩子正在喂自己的宝宝吃蚯蚓，妈妈给吓坏了。

她迅速打开窗子，向他们叫道："不要给他吃蚯蚓！他会生病的！"

孩子们一脸困惑地抬起头问道："昨天他生病啦？"

☆ **horrified** /ˈhɒrɪfaɪd/ *a*. 感到恐惧的，惊骇的

51

Help Me Ring the Bell

Walking down the street, a man passes a house and notices a little boy trying to reach the doorbell. No matter how much the little guy stretches, he can't make it.

The man calls out, "Let me get that for you," and he bounds onto the porch to ring the bell.

"Thanks, mister," says the kid, "Now let's run!"

帮我按门铃

一个人走在街上，路过一座房子时，他注意到一个小男孩在使劲够门铃。可是无论他怎样使劲都够不着。

那个人说道："让我来帮你吧。"然后他跳进门廊，按响了门铃。

"谢谢你，先生。现在，咱们赶快跑吧！"

☆ **stretch** /stretʃ/ *v.* 舒展；伸长

☆ **bound** /baund/ *v.* 跳跃

☆ **porch** /pɔːtʃ/ *n.* （建筑物前有顶的）

门廊

Why Two Holes?

One warm spring afternoon, a mother was playing in the yard with her two young children.

Her three-year-old daughter asked her why there were two holes in their nose.

Her four-year-old son quickly responded with, "So you can still breathe when you pick your nose!"

为什么有两个洞？

一个和煦的春日下午，妈妈正在院子里和一双小儿女玩耍。

三岁的女儿问她为什么人长有两个鼻孔。

四岁的儿子马上答道："这样你挖鼻孔时，还有另一个在喘气！"

☆ respond /rɪˈspɒnd/ *v.* 回答；做出反应

☆ pick one's nose 掏鼻子

Claim a Reward

A lady lost her handbag in the bustle of Christmas shopping.

It was found by an honest little boy and returned to her.

Looking in her purse, she commented, "Hmmm. . . . That's funny. When I lost my bag there was a $ 20 bill in it. Now there are twenty $ 1 bills."

The boy quickly replied, "That's right, lady. The last time I found a lady's purse, she didn't have any change for a reward!"

讨要赏赐

一位女士在圣诞节大采购的忙乱中丢了手提包。

一个诚实的小男孩捡到了还给她。

女士检查了钱包后，说道："真有意思，丢之前我的包里有一张 20 块钱的钞票，现在变成了 20 张一块钱的。"

小男孩马上答道："是这样的，女士。上次我捡到一位女士的钱包时，她就没有零钱奖励我！"

☆ **bustle** /ˈbʌsl/ *n.* 忙乱；喧扰

☆ **comment** /ˈkɒment/ *v.* 评论，发表意见

☆ **change** /tʃeɪndʒ/ *n.* 零钱；小额纸币（或硬币）

☆ **reward** /rɪˈwɔːd/ *n.* 报答；酬金；奖赏

Who Is God?

A confused little boy goes up to his mother and asks, "Is God male or female?"

After thinking for a moment, his mother responds, "Well, God is both male and female."

This confuses the little boy, so he asks, "Is God black or white?"

His mother smiled and answered, "Well, God is both black and white."

This further confuses the boy so he asks, "Is God gay or straight?"

上帝是谁？

一个困惑的小男孩去问他的妈妈："上帝是男人还是女人？"

想了一会儿，妈妈答道："既是男人也是女人。"

这让小男孩更加困惑了，于是他又问道："那么上帝是白人还是黑人？"

妈妈笑着回答说："这个吗，既是白人也是黑人。"

小男孩更不能理解了："那上帝是不是同性恋呢？"

At this the mother is getting concerned, but answers nonetheless, "Honey, God is both gay and straight."

At this the boy's face lights up with understanding and he triumphantly asks, "Is God Michael Jackson?"

对于这个问题，妈妈有些担心，但是她仍然答道："既是也不是，宝贝。"

这下，小男孩一脸"我明白了"的喜色，得意洋洋地问道："上帝是迈克尔·杰克逊吧？"

☆ **confuse** /kən'fjuːz/ *v.* 把（某人）弄糊涂；使迷惑

☆ **further** /'fɜːðə(r)/ *ad.* 进一步地

☆ **gay** /geɪ/ *a.* 同性恋的

☆ **straight** /streɪt/ *a.* 非同性恋的

☆ **nonetheless** /ˌnʌnðə'les/ *ad.* 仍然，不过

☆ **triumphantly** /traɪ'ʌmfəntlɪ/ *ad.* 胜利地；（因胜利或成功）欢欣鼓舞地；洋洋得意地

Why Are Some Hairs White?

One day, a little girl is sitting and watching her mother wash the dishes in the kitchen.

She suddenly notices that her mother has several strands of white hair sticking out in contrast to her brunette hair.

She looks at her mother and inquisitively asks, "Why are some of your hairs white, Mom?"

为什么一些头发是白色的?

一天，一个小姑娘正站在厨房里看着妈妈洗碗碟。

她突然注意到妈妈的一头黑发中伸出了几缕白发。

她看着妈妈好奇地问道："妈妈，为什么你有白头发?"

63

Her mother stroked her hair and replied, "Well, every time that you do something wrong and make me cry or unhappy, one of my hairs turns white."

The little girl thought about this revelation for a while and then asked, "Momma, how come all of grandma's hairs are white?"

妈妈摸了摸她的头发，答道："是这样的，每一次你做了错事惹我不高兴甚至把我气哭的时候，我的一根头发就会变成白色。"

小姑娘想了一会儿后又问道："妈妈，姥姥的满头头发是怎么都变白的呢？"

☆ **strand** /strænd/ *n.* 股；缕；绞

☆ **brunette** /bruːˈnet/ *a.* 黑色的；深褐色的

☆ **stroke** /strəuk/ *v.* （用手）轻抚

☆ **inquisitively** /ɪnˈkwɪzətɪvlɪ/ *ad.* 好奇地；爱钻研地

What Did God Do?

A woman went to the beach with her children.

Her 4-year-old son ran up to her, grabbed her hand, and led her to the shore where a dead seagull lay in the sand.

"Mommy, what happened to him?" the little boy asked.

"He died and went to heaven," she replied.

The child thought for a moment and said, "And God threw him back down?"

上帝做了什么？

妈妈带着孩子们去海滩上玩。

她四岁的儿子跑过来抓住她的手，带她来到岸边，沙滩上有一只死海鸥。

"妈妈，它怎么了？"小男孩问道。

"它死了，去天堂了，"她答道。

男孩想了一会儿说："然后，上帝又把它扔下来啦？"

Under the Wagon

A farm boy accidentally overturned his wagon loaded of corn. The farmer who lived nearby heard the noise.

"Hey Willis!!" the farmer yelled, "Forget your troubles. Come in with us. Then I'll help you get the wagon up."

"That's mighty nice of you," Willis answered, "but I don't think Pa would like me to."

"Aw, come on," the farmer insisted.

"Well okay," the boy finally agreed, and added, "but Pa won't like it."

在马车下面

农场的一个男孩不小心弄翻了装满玉米的马车。住在附近的农夫听到了动静。

"嗨,威利斯,"农夫叫道,"别管它了,过来和我们待会儿。一会儿我帮你把它弄起来。"

"您真是太好了,"威利斯答道,"但是我想爸爸不希望我这样做。"

"咳,来吧,"农夫坚持道。

"那么,好吧,"男孩最终同意了,可是又加上一句,"但是爸爸不会喜欢的。"

After a hearty dinner, Willis thanked his host, "I feel a lot better now, but I know Pa is going to be real upset."

"Don't be foolish!" the farmer said with a smile, "By the way, where is he?"

"Under the wagon!"

吃了丰盛的一餐后，男孩感谢热情的主人：
"我现在感觉好多了，但是我知道爸爸一定真的很
难过。"

"别傻了！"农夫笑着说，"顺便问一句，你爸
爸在哪儿？"

"在马车下面。"

71

What Does God Want?

A kitten was killed by a passing car right in front of a little boy.

The boy's grandfather buried the kitten behind the barn, and the grandmother distracted the boy by giving him cookies and orange juice.

While the little boy was eating, the following conversation took place.

"Grandma, what happened to the kitten?"

"It was killed by a car. The kitten is dead."

"Where does a kitten go when it dies?"

"God takes the kitten to heaven."

The little boy took another bite of cookie and then said, "But, Grandma, what does God want with a dead kitten?"

上帝想要什么?

一个小男孩亲眼目睹了一只小猫被过路的车轧死。

男孩的爷爷把猫埋在谷仓后面。奶奶给小男孩拿来饼干和橙汁,想要转移他的注意力。

小男孩吃东西的时候,和奶奶进行了下面的对话。

"奶奶,小猫怎么啦?"

"它被车撞了,它死啦。"

"小猫死了以后去哪儿了?"

"上帝带它去了天堂。"

小男孩又咬了一口饼干,说:"可是,奶奶,上帝要一只死了的小猫做什么呢?"

X-ray

A young girl was told she needed an X-ray. She went in the X-ray room and seemed especially nervous.

When she came out, she told her mother, "They took a picture of my bones."

"Yes, dear," replied the mother. "Did everything go all right?"

"Sure," said the girl. "It was great! I didn't even have to take my skin off!"

X 光检查

一个小姑娘要做 X 光检查，她无比紧张地走进 X 光室。

她出来的时候告诉妈妈："他们给我的骨头拍了片子。"

"是的，宝贝，"妈妈问，"照出来都好吗？"

"当然，"小姑娘说，"太神了！我都不用把皮脱掉！"

Drink Like a Fish

A guy hosted a dinner party for people from work, including his boss.

All during the sit-down dinner, the host's three-year-old girl stared at her father's boss sitting across from her. The girl could hardly eat her food from staring.

The man checked his tie, felt his face for food, patted his hair in place, but nothing stopped her from staring at him.

He tried his best to just ignore her, but finally it was too much for him.

像鱼一样喝酒

一个人举办了一次晚宴招待同事，还有他的老板。

餐桌上他三岁的女儿被安排坐在他的老板对面。整个用餐期间，小姑娘一直目不转睛地盯着老板看，以至于她自己都顾不上吃东西了。

老板检查了自己的领带，抹了抹脸确保上面没有食物，又把头发梳理整齐。可是小姑娘还是不错眼珠地盯着他。

他试图不去理她，但是最终他受够了。

He asked her, "Why are you staring at me?"

Everyone at the table had noticed her behavior and the table went quiet for her response.

The little girl said, "My Daddy said you drink like a fish and I don't want to miss it!"

他问她："你为什么一直盯着我看？"

餐桌前的每个人都注意到了小姑娘奇怪的举动，人们安静下来等着听她的回答。

小姑娘说："我爸爸说你'像鱼一样喝酒'，我可不想错过！"

☆ **ignore** /ɪgˈnɔː(r)/ *v.* 不理；忽视

☆ **behavior** /bɪˈheɪvjə(r)/ *n.* 行为；举止

☆ **drink like a fish** 是一句俗语，意思是"大喝，牛饮"。

Church Service

A Sunday school teacher asked her little children, as they were on the way to church service, "And why do we need to be quiet in church?"

One bright little girl replied right away, "Because people are sleeping in there!"

礼 拜

在去教堂做礼拜的路上，主日学校的老师问她的小学生们："为什么我们在教堂里要保持安静？"

一个聪明的小姑娘立刻答道："因为人们要在教堂里睡觉！"

Adam's Suit

A little boy opened the big and old family Bible with fascination, looking at the old pages as he turned them.

Suddenly, something fell out of the Bible and he picked it up and looked at it closely.

It was an old leaf from a tree that has been pressed in between the pages.

"Momma, look what I found," the boy called out.

"What have you got there, dear?" his mother asked.

With astonishment in the young boy's voice he answered, "I think it's Adam's suit!!"

亚当的衣服

小男孩着迷地打开又大又厚的家传《圣经》，翻看那些古旧的纸页。

突然，什么东西从书中掉落，男孩把它拣起来仔细查看。

这是夹在书页间的一片年久的树叶。

"妈妈，看我找到了什么，"小男孩叫道。

"你发现了什么，宝贝？"

小男孩语带惊奇地答道："我想这是亚当的衣服！！"

☆ **fascination** /ˌfæsɪˈneɪʃən/ *n.* 令人着迷的事物

☆ **astonishment** /əˈstɒnɪʃmənt/ *n.* 惊讶；惊愕

God's Power

One Sunday morning a little girl in her Sunday best was running so she wouldn't be late for church.

As she ran she kept praying, "Dear God, please don't let me be late to church. Please don't let me be late to church. . . . "

And, as she was running she tripped and fell.

When she got back up she began praying again, "Please, God don't let me be late to church — but don't shove me either!"

上帝的力量

　　星期日的清晨，一个小姑娘穿着漂亮的衣服跑向教堂，以免迟到。

　　她一边跑一边祷告着："亲爱的上帝，请你不要让我迟到，请你不要让我迟到……"

　　她跑着跑着，突然绊了一跤。

　　她站起来时，又开始祈祷："上帝，请你不要让我迟到，可是，也请你不要推我！"

☆ **trip** /trɪp/ *v.* 绊；绊倒

☆ **shove** /ʃʌv/ *v.* 推，猛推

They Are My Feet!

A three-year-old put his shoes on by himself. His mother noticed the left shoe was on the right foot.

She said, "Son, your shoes are on the wrong feet!"

He looked up at her with a raised eyebrow and said, "Don't kid me, Mom, I know they're my feet."

它们是我的脚!

一个三岁的小孩自己穿上了鞋子。妈妈注意到他把左脚的鞋子穿到了右脚上。

她说:"孩子,你把鞋子穿错了脚。"

他竖起眉毛,抬起头看着她说:"别骗我了,妈妈,我知道那是我的脚。"

Poorest Preacher

After the church service, a little boy told the pastor he was going to give him a lot of money when he grew up.

"Well, thank you," the pastor replied, "but why?"

"Because my daddy says you're one of the poorest preachers we've ever had!"

最穷的牧师

在教堂做完礼拜后，一个小男孩对牧师说长大了要捐很多钱给他。

"那么，谢谢你啦，"牧师说，"可是，为什么呢？"

"因为我爸爸说你是我们这儿最'穷'的牧师之一啦！"

☆ poor 有"贫穷的"的意思，也有"能力差的，糟糕的"的意思，这里应是后者，译为"最差劲的牧师"。

Sign Your Name in the Dark

Son: Dad, can you write in the dark?

Father: I think so. What is it you want me to write?

Son: Your name on my report card.

在黑暗中签名

儿子：爸爸，你能在黑暗中写字吗？

父亲：我想可以吧。你想让我写什么呢？

儿子：在我的成绩报告单上写上你的名字。

Take Good Care
of My Baby Sister

A boy was taking care of his baby sister while his parents went to town shopping.

In the afternoon, he decided to go fishing and he had to take her along.

"I'll never do that again!" he told his mother that evening. "I didn't catch a thing!"

"Oh, next time I'm sure she'll be quiet and not scare the fish away," his mother said.

The boy said, "It wasn't that. She ate all the bait!"

好好照顾我的小妹妹

爸爸妈妈去城里买东西时，小男孩负责照顾自己的小妹妹。

下午，他决定去钓鱼，他不得不带着妹妹一起去。

"我再也不干了！"晚上他对妈妈抱怨道，"我什么也没钓到！"

"哦，我保证下一次妹妹一定会安安静静的，不会把鱼吓跑。"

"不是那个问题。事实上是她把所有的鱼饵都吃掉了！"

☆ **scare** /skeə(r)/ v. 使惊恐；吓走，吓跑

No Difference

Little Johnny returns from school and says he got an F in arithmetic.

"Why?" asks the father.

"The teacher asked 'How much is 2 × 3?' and I said '6'."

"But that's right!"

"Then she asked me 'How much is 3 × 2?'"

"What's the fucking difference?"

"That's exactly what I said!"

没有区别

小约翰尼放学回到家里，告诉爸爸说他算术课不及格。

"为什么呀?"爸爸问道。

"老师问'2 乘 3 得多少?'，我说'得6'。"

"没错啊!"

"然后她又问'3 乘 2 得多少?'。"

"这该死的有什么区别?"

"我就是这么说的!"

☆ **arithmetic** /əˈrɪθmətɪk/ *n.* 算术；四则

Pull Through

"I've just had the most awful time," complained a boy to his friends.

"First I got angina pectoris, then arteriosclerosis. Just as I was recovering, I got psoriasis. They gave me hypodermics, and to top it all, tonsillitis was followed by appendectomy."

"Wow! How did you pull through?" sympathized his friends.

度过难关

"我刚度过了最难过的一段时光，"一个男孩在对他的朋友们诉苦。

"先是心绞痛，然后是动脉硬化。我才缓过劲来，牛皮癣又来了，还要皮下注射。最要命的是扁桃体炎和阑尾切除接踵而来。"

"天哪！你是怎么挺过来的？"朋友们同情地问道。

97

"I don't know," the boy replied. "Toughest spelling test I ever had."

"我也不知道,"男孩答道,"我做过的最难的拼写测验。"

☆ **awful** /'ɔːfʊl/ *a.* 难过的；使人极不舒服的

☆ **angina pectoris** /æn'dʒaɪnə 'pektərɪs/ *n.*【医】心绞痛

☆ **arteriosclerosis** /ɑːˌtɪərɪəʊsklɪə'rəʊsɪs/ *n.*【医】动脉硬化

☆ **psoriasis** /sɔ'raɪəsɪs/ *n.*【医】牛皮癣

☆ **hypodermic** /ˌhaɪpəʊ'dɜːmɪk/ *n.* 皮下注射

☆ **tonsillitis** /ˌtɒnsɪ'laɪtɪs/ *n.*【医】扁桃体炎

☆ **appendectomy** /ˌæpen'dektəmɪ/ *n.*【医】阑尾切除

☆ **pull through**　度过难关；恢复健康

Kids' Views on School

A little girl had just finished her first week of school.

"Mommy, I'm wasting my time," she said to her mother. "I can't read, I can't write — and they won't let me talk!"

孩子对学校的看法

一个小女孩刚上了一星期的学。

"妈妈，我在浪费时间，"她对妈妈说，"我不能读书，不能写字；他们还不让我说话。"

101

You Didn't Go to School When You Were Young?!

On the way home from the first day of school, the father asked his son, "What did you do at school today?"

The little boy shrugged his shoulders and said, "Nothing."

Hoping to draw his son into conversation, the father persisted and said, "Well, did you learn about any numbers, study certain letters, or maybe a particular color?"

The perplexed child looked at his father and said, "Daddy, didn't you go to school when you were a little boy?"

你·小·时候没上过学?!

儿子第一天上学，在放学回家的路上，爸爸问儿子："今天你在学校都做什么了？"

小男孩耸了耸肩膀说："没干什么。"

爸爸想拉儿子聊聊，于是继续问道："那么，你们有没有学认数字，或者学习一些新字，或者学习辨认一些颜色？"

困惑不解的小男孩看着爸爸问道："爸爸，你小的时候没上过学吗？"

☆ **persist** /pəˈsɪst/ *v.* 坚持不懈；执意

☆ **perplexed** /pəˈplekst/ *a.* 困惑的，茫然的

Pray for Gifts

Two young brothers were spending the night with their grandparents the week before Christmas. At bedtime, the two boys knelt beside their beds to say their prayers when the younger one began praying at the top of his lungs.

"I PRAY FOR A NEW BICYCLE . . ."

"I PRAY FOR A NEW NINTENDO . . ."

"I PRAY FOR A NEW MP3 . . ."

His older brother leaned over and nudged the younger brother and said, "Why are you shouting your prayers? God isn't deaf."

To which the little brother replied, "No, but Grandma is!"

祈求礼物

圣诞节前一周的晚上，小兄弟俩在爷爷奶奶家里过夜。临睡前，两个孩子跪在床前祷告祈求圣诞礼物。弟弟放声大叫着：

"我想要一辆新自行车……"

"我想要一个新游戏机……"

"我想要一款新的 MP3……"

哥哥侧身推推他说："你那么大声嚷嚷干吗？上帝又不聋。"

弟弟答道："上帝是不聋，奶奶的耳朵可不太好使！"

☆ at the top of one's lungs　用尽量大的声音

105

What Did He Say?

"Hey, Mom," asked little Johnny, "can you give me twenty dollars?"

"Certainly not."

"If you do," he went on, "I'll tell you what dad said to the maid when you were at the beauty shop."

His mother's ears perked up and, grabbing her purse, she handed over the money. "Well? What did he say?"

"He said, 'Hey, Marie, make sure you wash my socks tomorrow.'"

他说了什么？

"妈妈，"小约翰尼问道，"能给我 20 块钱吗？"

"当然不行。"

"如果你给我 20 块钱，"小约翰尼接着说道，"我就告诉你，你去美容院时爸爸对保姆说了什么。"

妈妈的耳朵竖了起来，抓起钱包，拿出 20 块钱给了小约翰尼。"好吧，他说了什么？"

"他说：'玛丽，明天记得把我的袜子洗了。'"

☆ perk /pɜːk/ v.（傲慢地、自信地或敏捷地）昂

起，竖起，翘起

Can I Trust You?

Little Johnny was walking down the beach, and he spied a woman sitting under a beach umbrella on the sand.

He walked up to her and asked, "Are you a Christian?"

"Yes." she replied.

"Do you read your Bible every day?"

She nodded her head, "Yes."

"Do you pray often?" the boy asked next, and again she answered, "Yes."

With that he asked his final question, "Will you hold my quarter while I go swimming?"

我能相信你吗？

　　小约翰尼走在海滩上，看到一个女人坐在沙滩伞下。

　　他走上前去问道："你是基督徒吗？"

　　"是的。"

　　"你每天都读《圣经》吗？"

　　她点点头说："是的。"

　　"你经常做祷告吗？"小约翰尼又问道。她再次回答："是的。"

　　小约翰尼最后问道："那么我去游泳时，你能帮我拿着我的 25 分币吗？"

The Proper Behavior

A priest at a parochial school, wanting to point out the proper behavior for church, was trying to elicit from the youngsters rules that their parents might give before taking them to a nice restaurant.

"Don't play with your food," one second-grader cited.

"Don't be loud," said another.

"And what rule do your parents give you before you go out to eat?" the priest inquired of one little boy.

Without batting an eye, the child replied, "Order something cheap."

正确的行为

教区学校的牧师想要给孩子们指明在教堂里应遵从的行为规范。他循循善诱地从父母对孩子们在高级餐厅里就餐时的行为要求入手，要孩子们说说。

"不要摆弄食物，"一个二年级的孩子答道。

"不要吵闹，"另一个说道。

"那么你的爸爸妈妈在山去吃饭前对你提出什么要求？"牧师问一个小男孩。

小男孩眼睛眨也不眨一下，答道："拣便宜的菜点。"

☆ **parochial** /pəˈrəʊkɪəl/ *a.* 堂区的；（学校）由宗教团体兴办的

☆ **elicit** /ɪˈlɪsɪt/ *v.* 引出，推导出

What's Sex?

A little girl returning home from his first day at school said to his mother, "Mom, what's sex?"

Her mother, who believed in all the most modern educational theories, gave her a detailed explanation.

When she had finished, the confused girl produced an enrolment form which she had brought home from school and said, "Yes, but how am I going to get all that into this one little square?"

什么是性？

一个小姑娘第一天上学后，回到家里，对妈妈说："妈妈，什么是性？"

她的妈妈是个相信现代的教育理论的人，于是给小姑娘做了详尽的解释。

她说完后，困惑的小姑娘拿出一张从学校带回来的表格，问道："你说的我都明白了，但是我怎么能在这么小的空格里填进这么多东西？"

☆ **enrolment** /ɪnˈrəʊlmənt/ *n.* 登记，注册；登记簿，名册

Disappointment

Little Johnny ran into the kitchen crying and cradling something in both hands.

"Mommy, my turtle is dead," Little Johnny told his mother as he held the turtle out to her.

His mother kissed him on the head, then said, "That's all right. We'll wrap him in tissue paper, put him in a little box, then have a nice burial ceremony in the backyard. After that, we'll go out for an ice cream soda, and then get you a new pet. I don't want you. . . ."

Her voice trailed off as she noticed the turtle move in his hands.

"Johnny, your turtle is not dead after all."

"Oh," Little Johnny said, "Can I kill it?"

失 望

小约翰尼哭着跑进厨房，两只手里捧着什么东西。

"妈妈，我的小乌龟死了，"小约翰尼把手伸到妈妈跟前说道。

妈妈吻了他的额头，说："这样吧，我们用纸巾把它包起来，放在一个小盒子里，然后在后院为它举行葬礼。之后，我带你去吃冰激凌苏打水，再给你买一只宠物。我不想让你……"

突然她发现乌龟在小约翰尼的手里动了，她的声音低了下来。

"约翰尼，你的乌龟还没有死呢。"

"啊，"小约翰尼说，"那么我能把它弄死吗？"

☆ **cradle** /'kreɪdl/ *v.*（放在摇篮里般地）抱（或背等）

☆ **trail off** 逐渐减弱；缩小

Play House

A little girl and a little boy were playing in the neighborhood park.

The girl approached the boy and said, "Hey, Tommy, wanna play house?"

He said, "Sure! What do you want me to do?"

The girl replied, "I want you to communicate."

He said to her, "That word is too big. I have no idea what it means."

The little girl smirked and said, "Perfect. You can be the husband."

玩 "过家家"

一个小姑娘和一个小男孩在街区公园里玩。

小女孩走近男孩说："嗨，汤米，想不想玩'过家家'？"

小男孩答道："好啊！你想让我做什么？"

小女孩说："我想让你交流。"

他对她说："这个词太大了，我不懂是什么意思。"

小女孩得意地笑着说："太棒了。你可以扮丈夫。"

☆ **approach** /ə'prəʊtʃ/ *v.* 靠近，接近

What Do You Mean?

A mother took her little boy to church. While in church the little boy said, "Mommy, I have to pee."

The mother said to the little boy, "It's not appropriate to say the word 'pee' in church. So, from now on whenever you have to 'pee' just tell me that you have to 'whisper.'"

The following Sunday, the little boy went to church with his father.

During the service, he said to his father, "Daddy, I have to whisper."

The father looked at him and said, "Okay, why don't you whisper in my ear."

你是什么意思？

妈妈带着她的小男孩去教堂。正在做礼拜的时候，小男孩对妈妈说："妈妈，我要尿尿。"

妈妈对小男孩说："在教堂里说'尿尿'不好，以后你想要尿尿的时候就说'我要说悄悄话'。"

下个星期天，小男孩和爸爸一起去教堂。

做礼拜时，他对爸爸说："爸爸，我要说悄悄话。"

爸爸看着他说："好吧，来对着爸爸的耳朵说吧。"

Did God Make You?

A little girl is sitting on her grandpa's lap and studying the wrinkles on his old face.

She gets up the nerve to rub her fingers over the wrinkles. Then she touches her own face and looks more puzzled.

Finally the little girl asks, "Grandpa, did God make you?"

"He sure did honey, a long time ago," replies her grandpa.

上帝造的你吗？

小女孩坐在爷爷的大腿上，好奇地探究着他脸上的皱纹。

她紧张地摸索着爷爷的皱纹，然后又摸摸自己的脸，她看上去很困惑。

终于，她忍不住问道："爷爷，是上帝造的你吗？"

"当然啦，好久以前了，"爷爷答道。

121

"Well, did God make me?" asks the little girl.

"Yes, He did, and that wasn't too long ago," answers her grandpa.

"Boy," says the little girl, "He's sure doing a lot better job these days, isn't He?"

"那么，是上帝造的我吗？"小女孩又问。

"是的，是上帝造了你，在不久以前，"爷爷答道。

"好家伙，"小女孩说，"近来上帝的活儿干得好多了，不是吗？"

☆ **wrinkle** /'rɪŋkl/ *n.* 皱纹；褶皱

123

I Don't Know Who You Are

"Isn't the principal a dummy!" said a boy to a girl.

"Say, do you know who I am?" asked the girl.

"No."

"I'm the principal's daughter."

"And do you know who I am?" asked the boy.

"No," she replied.

"Thank goodness!"

我不认识你

"校长真是个笨蛋，是吧！"男孩对女孩说。

"喔，你知道我是谁吗？"女孩问道。

"不知道。"

"我是校长的女儿。"

"那么你认识我吗？"男孩问道。

"不认识。"

"感谢上帝！"

Go Slow

Father: Why were you late for school this morning, Joseph?

Joseph: Because of a sign down the road.

Father: What does a sign have to do with your being late?

Joseph: The sign said, "School Ahead, Go Slow!"

慢 慢 走

父亲：约瑟夫，今天早上你为什么上学迟到了？

约瑟夫：因为路上的一块指示牌。

父亲：指示牌和你上学迟到有什么关系？

约瑟夫：那是因为指示牌上写着"前方学校，减速慢行！"

I'm 6 Today

My Next-door Neighbor: Jack, how old are you on your last birthday?

My Son Jack: 5 years old.

Neighbor: How old are you going to be on your next birthday?

Jack: 7 years old.

Neighbor: That's impossible!

Jack: No it's not. I'm 6 today.

今天我6岁了

我隔壁的邻居：杰克，你上一次过生日时多大了？

我的儿子杰克：5岁。

邻居：那你下一次过生日时该几岁啦？

杰克：7岁。

邻居：这不可能！

杰克：不，是可能的。今天是我6岁的生日。

This Is My Father

The telephone rings in the principal's office at a school.

"Hello, this is No. 3 Elementary School," answers the principal.

"Hi. Jimmy won't be able to come to school all next week," replies the voice.

"Well, what seems to be the problem with him?"

"We are all going on a family vacation," says the voice, "I hope it is all right."

"I guess that would be fine," says the principal. "May I ask who is calling?"

"Sure. This is my father!"

我是我爸爸

校长办公室里的电话铃响了。

"你好，第三小学，"校长接电话。

"你好，下星期吉米一周都不能去上课，"电话那端说道。

"他有什么事情吗？"

"我们全家要去度假，我希望这没什么问题。"

"我想这没问题，"校长答道，"请问您是哪位？"

"哦，是我爸爸！"

The Ten Most Wanted Men

Little Johnny's kindergarten class was on a field trip to the local police station, where they saw pictures of the 10 Most Wanted men tacked to a bulletin board.

One of the youngsters pointed to a picture and asked if it really was the photo of a wanted person.

"Yes," said the policeman. "The detectives want him very badly."

So Little Johnny asked, "Why didn't you keep him when you took his picture?"

十个被紧急通缉的人

小约翰尼上的幼儿园带孩子们去警察局参观。在那里他们看到布告板上钉着 10 个被紧急通缉的人的照片。

一个孩子指着一张照片问是不是确实是那个被通缉的人的照片。

"是的,"警察答道,"警察叔叔们太想抓到他了。"

小约翰尼问道:"那你们给他照相时干吗不抓住他呢?"

Picture of God

A nursery school teacher was observing her class of children while they drew.

She would occasionally walk around to see each child's artwork.

As she got to one little girl who was working diligently, she asked what the drawing was.

The girl replied, "I'm drawing God."

The teacher paused and said, "But no one knows what God looks like."

Without looking up from her drawing, the girl replied, "They will in a minute."

上帝的画像

幼儿园的孩子们在画画时，老师在旁边巡视。

她个时地走来走去看孩子们的画作。

当她注意到一个小姑娘在极其细致认真地作画时，她问她在画什么。

小姑娘答道："我在画上帝。"

老师顿了一下说："可是没有人知道上帝长什么样子。"

小姑娘头也不抬一下地答道："马上就会知道了。"

☆ **occasionally** /əˈkeɪʒənəlɪ/ *ad.* 偶然，偶尔

135

Nightgown

Little Suzie was in her bedroom when her younger brother knocked on the door.

"Hey, Suzie, Let me in!" he shouted.

"I can't let you in because I'm in my nightgown and mama says it isn't right for little boys to see little girls in their nightgowns!"

Her little brother thought about this for a moment, then turned to walk away, when Suzie called out from her room. "You can come in now! I took it off!"

睡 衣

小苏茜在卧室里，她的小弟弟来敲门。

"嗨，苏茜，让我进去！"他嚷道。

"我不能让你进来，因为我穿着睡衣。妈妈说了，女生不应该让男生看见穿着睡衣！"

小弟弟想了一会儿后，转身走了。这时小苏茜在屋里叫道："现在你可以进来了，我把睡衣脱了！"

137

Where Are My Boots?

There was a little boy in kindergarten. He cried, so the teacher asked him what was wrong.

He sobbed, "I can't find my boots."

The teacher looked around the classroom and saw a pair of boots, "Are these yours?"

"No, they're not mine," the boy shook his head.

The teacher and the boy searched all over the classroom for his boots.

Finally, the teacher gave up, "Are you SURE those boots are not yours?"

"I'm sure," the boy sobbed, "mine had snow on them."

138

我的靴子哪儿去了?

幼儿园里有一个小男孩哭了，老师过来问他怎么了。

他抽噎着说："我的靴子找不到了。"

老师在教室里找了一圈，看到一双靴子问他："这双是你的吗?"

"不是的，"小男孩摇摇头。

老师又带着男孩到处找了一遍。

最后，老师停下来问："你确定这双靴子不是你的?"

"肯定不是，"小男孩哭着说，"我的靴子上面有雪。"

139

He Won

Little Tommy and Little Johnny are playing in the backyard.

Tommy: How's your little brother, Johnny?

Johnny: He's ill in bed. He hurt himself.

Tommy: That's too bad. How did it happen?

Johnny: Well, we betted who could lean further out of the window, and he won.

他赢了

小汤米和小约翰尼在院子里玩。

汤米：约翰尼，你弟弟怎么啦？

约翰尼：他病了，在床上躺着呢。他把自己弄伤了。

汤米：那可太糟糕了。他是怎么搞的？

约翰尼：呃，我们打赌谁能把身子探出窗子更多，他赢了。

Your Worries Are Over

Young Girl: Mommy, remember that vase you always worried I would break?

Her Mom: Of course. What about it?

Young Girl: Your worries are over.

你不用再担心了

小女孩：妈妈，你还记得你总是担心我会打破的那只花瓶吗？

她的妈妈：当然，怎么啦？

小女孩：你不用再担心了。

Bed Time

One night a father sent his son to bed.

Five minutes later the boy screamed, "Dad! Can you get me a glass of water!?!"

"No."

A minute later the boy screamed, "Dad!! Can you get me a glass of water?"

"No. Next time you ask I'll come up there and spank your bottom."

"Dad! When you come up to spank my bottom, can you bring me a glass or water?"

睡觉时间

一天晚上，爸爸把儿子送上床睡觉。

五分钟以后，小男孩叫起来："爸爸，你能不能帮我拿杯水来？！"

"不行。"

一会儿，孩子又叫道："爸爸，你能不能帮我拿杯水来？！"

"不行，我再听你叫一声，我就来打你屁股。"

"爸爸，你来打我屁股的时候，能不能帮我带杯水来？"

☆ **spank** /spæŋk/ *v.* （用手掌、拖鞋等）掴，拍打

（尤指打屁股）

145

He Shaves 50 Times a Day!

Little Harry and Little Henry are sitting on the grass in the garden, bragging about their big brothers.

Harry: My big brother shaves every day.

Henry: My brother shaves fifty times a day!

Harry: That's impossible!

Henry: No, it's not. He's a barber.

他每天刮 50 次脸！

小哈里和小亨利坐在花园里的草地上，拿自己的哥哥吹牛。

哈里：我哥哥每天都刮脸。

亨利：我哥哥每天刮 50 次脸。

哈里：这个可能。

亨利：怎么不可能。他是理发师。

☆ **brag** /bræg/ *v.* 自夸，吹嘘

147

A Big Tiger

Tom: I went for a walk in a large park last week. It was very cold and the wind was blowing hard. All of a sudden, I saw a big tiger....

Henry: Oh, what did you do then?

Tom: I looked at him for a while, then I put my hands into my pockets and went back home.

Henry: Did the tiger run after you?

Tom: No, he didn't of course. You see, it was shut in a cage.

一只大老虎

汤姆：上星期我去一个好大的公园玩。天很冷，风特大。突然，我看到一只大老虎……

亨利：天啊，你怎么办了？

汤姆：我看了它一会儿，然后把手插进口袋里回家了。

亨利：老虎追你了吗？

汤姆：当然没有，它关在笼子里。

149

Why Firemen Have Dogs

A kindergarten teacher was delivering a station wagon full of kids home one day when a fire truck zoomed past.

Sitting in the front seat of the fire truck was a Dalmatian dog.

The children fell to discussing the dog's duties.

"They use him to keep crowds back," said one youngster.

"No," said another, "he's just for good luck."

150

消防员为什么要带狗

一天，幼儿园老师在送一大客车的孩子们回家，路上，一辆消防车呼啸而过。

消防车的前座上坐着一只大斑点狗。

孩子们开始讨论起这只狗的作用。

一个孩子说："他们用它来不让人群靠近。"

"不对，"另一个说，"他是只幸运狗，他们带着它只是为了好运。"

A third child brought the argument to a close.

"They use the dogs," she said firmly, "to find the fire hydrant."

第三个孩子的话使争论停了下来。

"他们带着狗，"她肯定地说，"是用来找消防栓的。"

☆ zoom /zu:m/ v. 嗡嗡（或隆隆）地疾行

☆ Dalmatian /dæl'meɪʃjən/ n. 达尔马提亚狗（一种白色黑斑或棕斑的短毛大狗）

☆ hydrant /'haɪdrənt/ n. 给水栓；消防栓，消防龙头

He Will Follow Us

Realizing that their home was just not big enough with the new baby in the house, Little Johnny's parents discussed moving to a bigger one.

Little Johnny sat patiently listening to his parents.

Finally, he piped in, "It's no use. He'll just follow us anyway."

他会跟着我们

小约翰尼的爸爸妈妈又生了一个小宝宝，他们意识到现在的房子不够大了，他们讨论着要搬个大一些的房子。

小约翰尼耐着性子听他们说。

终于，他插进来说："没用的，不管怎么样他都会一直跟着我们的。"

Ask Your Father

The family was on a trip and the 3-year-old son was merrily singing songs.

After a while he asked, "Mommy, sing with me?"

The mother answered no, she didn't want to.

Well, the little boy kept pestering her to sing until finally she said, "Ask your father!"

"Dad," said the little tyke. "Will you tell mom to sing with me?"

问你爸爸

一家人在旅行途中，三岁的儿子一直欢快地唱着歌。

过了一会儿，他问道："妈妈，跟我一块儿唱歌，好吗？"

妈妈说不，她不想唱歌。

然而，小伙子一直缠着她要她唱。终于，她说："去问你爸爸！"

"爸爸，"这个小淘气包说，"你能不能让妈妈和我一块儿唱歌？"

☆ **merrily** /ˈmerɪlɪ/ *ad.* 愉快地，快乐地

☆ **pester** /ˈpestə(r)/ *v.* 不断打扰，纠缠

☆ **tyke** /taɪk/ *n.* 〈口〉小孩子；小淘气

He Doesn't Have Kids

My little nephew was explaining to me that his father's friend was deaf and had to speak with his hands.

I asked my nephew how his father's friend shouted in sign language.

His reply, "He doesn't have to, he doesn't have any kids."

他没有小孩

我的小外甥在和我讲他爸爸的一个朋友是聋哑人，不得不用手语与人交流。

我问小外甥他爸爸的这个朋友怎么用手语对别人大喊大叫。

他答道："他不用对人大喊大叫，他没有孩子。"

Nickel or Dime?

Little Johnny used to hang out at the local corner store.

The owner didn't know what Johnny's problem was, but the older boys would constantly tease him.

They would play a game with him, sometimes they would offer Johnny his choice between a nickel (5 cents) and a dime (10 cents) in their open palms and Johnny would always take the nickel — they said, because it was bigger.

五分钱还是十分钱？

小约翰尼过去常在街角的商店附近闲逛。

店主不知道小约翰尼有什么问题，但是年龄大些的男孩子们经常嘲弄他。

他们和他玩一种游戏作弄他，有时他们在掌心上放一个五分镍币和一个十分硬币让约翰尼选。约翰尼总是选五分的——他们说是因为五分镍币个儿大。

161

One day after Johnny grabbed the nickel, the store owner took him aside and said, "Johnny, those boys are making fun of you. Don't you know that a dime is twice as good as a nickel? Are you grabbing the nickel because it's bigger, or what?"

Slowly, Johnny turned toward the storeowner and a big grin appeared on his face and Johnny said, "Well, if I took the dime, they'd stop doing it, and so far I have saved $20!"

一天，在约翰尼又拿了五分镍币后，店主把他叫到一边问："约翰尼，那些孩子在作弄你。你不知道十分硬币要值两个五分镍币吗？你选五分镍币是因为它大吗？"

约翰尼慢吞吞转向店主，咧嘴笑着说："是这样的，如果我拿了十分硬币，他们就不会再跟我玩了。事实上，到现在我已经赚了20块钱了！"

☆ **tease** /tiːz/ *v.* 戏弄；取笑

☆ **nickel** /ˈnɪkəl/ *n.* （美国和加拿大的）5分镍币

☆ **dime** /daɪm/ *n.* （美国和加拿大的）10分铸币

☆ **make fun of somebody** 拿某人开玩笑，取笑某人

Greatest Hitter in the World

A little boy strutted through the backyard, wearing his baseball cap and toting a ball and bat.

"I'm the greatest hitter in the world," he announced.

Then, he tossed the ball into the air, swung at it, and missed.

"Strike One!" he yelled.

Undaunted, he picked up the ball and said again, "I'm the greatest hitter in the world!"

He tossed the ball into the air. When it came down he swung again and missed.

"Strike Two!"

世界上最棒的击球手

　　一个小男孩戴着棒球帽、背着棒球和球棒在后院里昂首阔步地走过。

　　"我是世界上最棒的击球手，"他宣布说。

　　然后，他把球抛到半空中，挥动球棒，没击中。

　　"一击！"他叫道。

　　他不屈不挠地捡起球，又说道："我是世界上最棒的击球手！"

　　他把球抛到空中，球落下时挥动球棒，没击中。

　　"二击！"

The boy then paused a moment to examine his bat and ball carefully.

He spit on his hands and rubbed them together.

He straightened his cap and said once more, "I'm the greatest hitter in the world!"

Again he tossed the ball up in the air and swung at it. He missed.

"Strike Three!"

"Wow!" he exclaimed. "I'm the greatest PITCHER in the world!"

这回，男孩停下来仔细地检查了球和球棒。

　　他往手心里吐了唾沫，搓了搓。

　　他正了正自己的棒球帽，又说了一遍："我是世界上最棒的击球手！"

　　他再次把球抛到空中，挥动球棒，没击中。

　　"三击！"

　　"哇噢！"他激动地叫道，"我是世界上最棒的投手！"

☆ **strut** /strʌt/ v. 趾高气昂地走，高视阔步

☆ **tote** /təut/ v. （手）提；（背）负

☆ **announce** /əˈnauns/ v. 宣布，宣告；声称

☆ **toss** /tɒs/ v. 扔，抛，掷

☆ **swing** /swɪŋ/ v. （swung, swung）挥动拳头（或
　　手臂、棍棒）打击

☆ **undaunted** /ˌʌnˈdɔːntɪd/ a. 大胆的，勇敢的

☆ **straighten** /ˈstreɪtən/ v. 使平正；整理

Thank You, Lord

A 4-year-old boy was asked to return thanks before Thanksgiving dinner. The family members bowed their heads in expectation.

He began his prayer, thanking the Lord for all his friends, naming them one by one.

Then he thanked the Lord for Mommy, Daddy, brother, sister, Grandma, Grandpa, and all his aunts and uncles.

Then he began to thank the Lord for the food. He gave thanks for the turkey, the dressing, the fruit salad, the cranberry sauce, the pies, the cakes, even the Cool Whip.

感谢上帝

感恩节时，一个四岁的小男孩要做餐前感恩祈祷。全家人低着头，期待着。

他开始祷告，他代朋友们对上帝感恩，并挨个提到他们的名字。

然后，他代妈妈、爸爸、兄弟姐妹、爷爷、奶奶，还有所有的叔叔、阿姨对上帝感恩。

然后，他感谢上帝赐予他的食物，从火鸡、火鸡填馅，到水果沙拉、橘酱，各种点心、蛋糕，甚至冰蛋奶水果，一一列举。

Then he paused, and everyone waited —
and waited.

After a long silence, the young fellow
looked up at his mother and asked, "If I thank
the Lord for the broccoli, won't He know that I'm
lying?"

然后，他停了下来，大家都等着听他继续，等啊等。

　　好久之后，小伙子抬起头看着妈妈问道："如果我感谢上帝赐予我花椰菜，上帝会不会知道我在说谎？"

　　☆ **expectation** /ˌekspekˈteɪʃən/ *n.* 期待；预期
　　☆ **cranberry** /ˈkrænbərɪ/ *n.* 【植】越橘；越橘的果实
　　☆ **broccoli** /ˈbrɒkəlɪ/ *n.* 【植】花椰菜，球花甘蓝